THE MOTHER
ON
HERSELF

SRI AUROBINDO ASHRAM
PONDICHERRY

First Edition 1977
Second Impression 1981
Second Edition 1989
Fourth Impression 2001

ISBN 81-7058-172-9

© Sri Aurobindo Ashram Trust 1977, 1989
Published by Sri Aurobindo Ashram Publication Department
Printed at Sri Aurobindo Ashram Press, Pondicherry

PRINTED IN INDIA

The extracts for this book have been selected from the Mother's own writings. A list of references is given on pages 43-44. A chronology of incidents in the Mother's external life appears on pages 45-46.

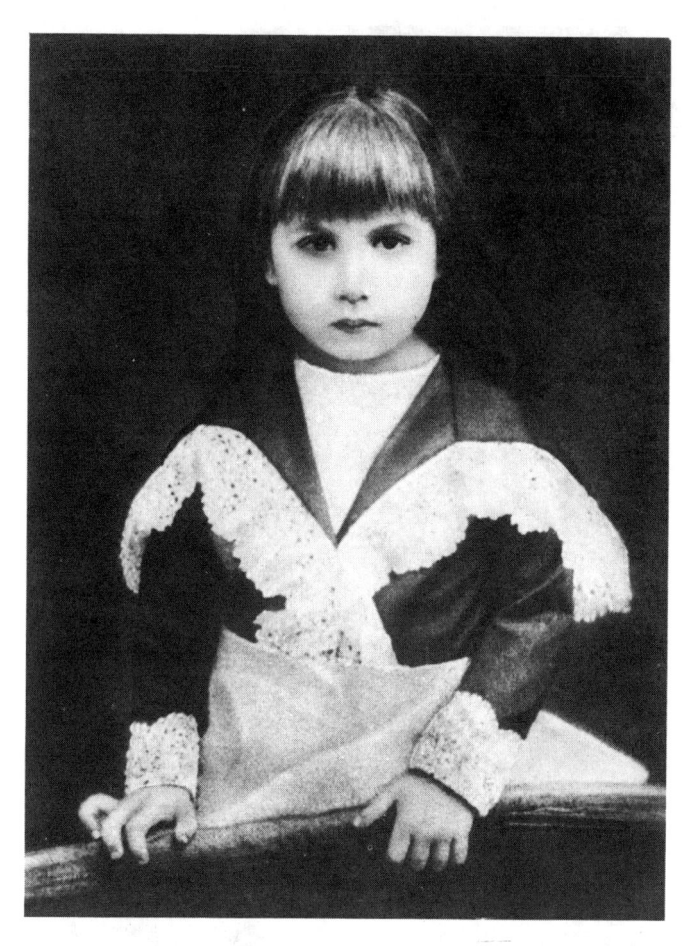

The Mother, age seven, 1885

The Mother
Durga Puja, 5.10.1954

Do not ask questions about the details of the material existence of this body; they are in themselves of no interest and must not attract attention.

Throughout all this life, knowingly or unknowingly, I have been what the Lord wanted me to be, I have done what the Lord wanted me to do. That alone matters.

When and how did I become conscious of a mission which I was to fulfil on earth?... It is difficult to say when it came to me. It is as though I were born with it, and following the growth of the mind and brain, the precision and completeness of this consciousness grew also.

*

From the age of five I was conscious that I did not belong to this world, that I did not have a human consciousness. My sadhana began at that age.

*

Whatever the way we follow, the subject we study, we always arrive at the same result. The most important thing for an individual is to unify himself around his divine centre; in that way he becomes a true individual, master of himself and his destiny.... But if you are consciously organised, unified around the divine centre, ruled and directed by it, you are master of your destiny. That is worth the trouble of attempting.... In any case, I find it preferable to be the master rather than the slave. It is a rather unpleasant sensation to feel yourself pulled by the strings and made to do things whether you want to or not — that is quite irrelevant — but to be compelled to act because something pulls you by the strings, something which you do not even see — that is exasperating. However, I do not know, but I found it very exasperating, even when I was quite a child. At five, it began to seem to me quite intolerable and I sought for a way so that it might be otherwise — without people getting a chance to scold me. For I knew nobody who could help me and I did not have the chance that you have, someone who can tell you: "This is what you have to do!" There was nobody to tell me that. I had to find it out all by myself. And I found it. I started at five.

*

You have never thought about it? You have never looked into yourself to see what effect you exercise upon yourself? Never thought over it?... Never tried to understand how you feel?... Never sought to understand how, for example, decisions take place in you? From where do they come? What makes you decide one thing rather than another? And what is the relation between a decision of yours and your action? And to what extent do you have the freedom of choice between one thing and another? And how far do you feel you are able to, you are free to do this or that or that other or nothing at all?...You have pondered over that?...

I was preoccupied with that when I was a child of five!...

This happened to me.... I was five or six or seven years old (at seven the thing became quite serious) and I had a father who loved the circus, and he came and told me: "Come with me, I am going to the circus on Sunday." I said: "No, I am doing something much more interesting than going to the circus!" Or again, young friends invited me to attend a meeting where we were to play together, enjoy together: "No, I enjoy here much more...." And it was quite sincere. It was not a pose: for me, it was like this, it was true. There was nothing in the world more enjoyable than that.

*

From my earliest childhood I have not stopped observing things. When I was very young I was chided for never speaking. It was because I spent my time observing. I passed my time observing, I registered everything, I learnt all I could, I did not stop learning.... I have seen a great number of people, I began attending to people when very young, I have seen many countries,... in every country I lived the life of that country in order to understand it well, and there is nothing which interested me in my outer being as much as learning.

*

[When I was a child] I was exclusively occupied with my studies — finding things out, learning, understanding, knowing. That was my interest, even my passion. My mother, who loved us very much — my brother and myself — never allowed us to be ill tempered or discontented or lazy. If we went to complain to her about one thing or another, to tell her that we were discontented, she would make fun of us or scold us and say, "What is this nonsense? Don't be ridiculous. Quick! off you go and work, and never mind whether your are in a good or bad mood! That is of no interest at all."

My mother was perfectly right and I have always been very grateful to her for having taught me the discipline and the necessity of self-forgetfulness through concentration on what one is doing.

*

I suggest the same remedy as the one I was using in my childhood when disagreeing with my young playmates. I was at that time...very sensitive and I felt hurt when abused by them, especially by those to whom I had shown only sympathy and kindness. I used to tell myself: "Why be sorry and feel miserable? If they are right in what they say, I have only to be glad for the lesson and correct myself; if they are wrong, why should I worry about it — it is for them to be sorry for their mistake. In both cases the best and the most dignified thing I can do is to remain strong, quiet and unmoved."

This lesson which I was giving myself and trying to follow when I was eight years old, still holds good in all similar cases.

*

I remember having learnt to play tennis when I was eight, it was a passion; but I never wished to play with my little comrades because I learnt nothing (usually I used to defeat them), I always went to the best players. At times they looked surprised, but in the end they played with me — I never won but I learnt much.

*

I was scolded all the time because I did many different things. And I was always told I would never be good at anything. I studied, I did painting, I did music, and then was busy with still other things. And I was told my music wouldn't be up to much, my painting wouldn't be worthwhile, and that my studies would be quite incomplete. Probably it is quite true, but still I have found that this had its advantages — those very advantages I am speaking about, of widening, making supple one's mind and understanding. It is true that if I had wanted to be a first-class player and to play in concerts, it would have been necessary to do what they said. And as for painting, if I had wanted to be among the great artists of the period, it would have been necessary to do that. That's quite understandable. But still, that is just one point of view. I don't see any necessity of being the greatest artist, the greatest musician. That has always seemed to me a vanity.

*

There are children who know how to do this, they continue their dreams. Every evening when they go to bed they return to the same place and continue their dream....

Nothing is more interesting. It is a most pleasant way of passing the nights. You begin a story, then, when it is time to wake up, you put a full stop to the last sentence and come back into your body. And then the following night you start off again, re-open the page and resume your story during the whole time you are out; and then you arrange things well — they must be well arranged, it must be very beautiful. And when it is time to come back, you put a full stop once again and tell those things, "Stay very quiet till I return!" And you come back into your body. And you continue this every evening and write a book of wonderful fairy-tales — provided you remember them when you wake up....

When I was small I used to call this "telling stories to oneself." It is not at all a telling with words, in one's head: it is a going away to this place which is fresh and pure, and...building up a wonderful story there. And if you know how to tell yourself a story in this way, and if it is truly beautiful, truly harmonious, truly powerful and well coordinated, this story will be realised in your life — perhaps not exactly in the form in which you created it, but as a more or less changed physical expression of what you made.

That may take years, perhaps, but your story will tend to organise your life.

But there are very few people who know how to tell a beautiful story; and then they always mix horrors in it, which they regret later.

If one could create a magnificent story without any horror in it, nothing but beauty, it would have a *considerable* influence on everyone's life. And this is what people don't know.

*

I practised occultism when I was twelve. But I must say I had no fear — I feared nothing. One goes out of one's body, one is tied by something resembling an almost imperceptible thread — if the thread is cut, it is all over. Life also is ended. One goes out, and then one can begin seeing the world where one has gone. And usually the first things one sees, as I said, are terrifying. Because, for you the air is empty, there is nothing in it — you see something blue or white, there are clouds, sunbeams, and all that is very pretty — but when you have the other sight, you see that it is filled with a multitude of small formations which are all residues of desires or of mental deformations and these swarm in there, you know, in a mass, and this is not always quite pretty. At times it is extremely ugly. This assails you — it comes, presses upon you, attacks you — and if you are afraid, it takes absolutely frightful forms.

Naturally, if you do not flinch, if you can look upon all that with a healthy curiosity, you perceive that it is not at all so terrifying. It may not be pretty, but is not terrifying.

I could tell you a little story.

I knew a Danish painter who was quite talented and who wanted to learn occultism (moreover, he had come here, had met Sri Aurobindo; he had even done his portrait — that was during the war), and when he came back to France, he wanted me to teach him a little of this occult science. I taught him how to go out of his body etc., and the controls, all that. And I told him that above all, the first thing was not to have any fear. Then, one day he came to tell me that he had had a dream that night. But it was not a dream, for, as I have told you, he knew a bit how to go out of his body, and he had gone out consciously. And once he had gone out he was looking around seeing what was to be seen, when suddenly, he saw a formidable tiger coming towards him, drawing close with the most frightful intentions.... He remembered what I had told him, that he must not be afraid. So he began to say to himself: "There is no danger, I am protected, nothing can happen to me, I am wrapped up in the power of protection", and he began looking at the tiger in that way, without any fear. And as he went on looking at the tiger, immediately it started growing smaller and smaller and smaller, and it became a tiny little cat!

*

When I began studying occultism, I became aware that — just when I began to work upon my nights in order to make them conscious — I became aware that there was between the subtle-physical and the most material vital a small region, very small, which was not sufficiently developed to serve as a conscious link between the two activities. So what took place in the consciousness of the most material vital did not get translated exactly in the consciousness of the most subtle physical. Some of it got lost on the way because it was like a — not positively a void but something only half-conscious, not sufficiently developed. I knew there was only one way, that was to work to develop it. I began working. This happened sometime about the month of February, I believe. One month, two months, three, four, no result. We go on. Five months, six months...it was at the end of July or the beginning of August...I left Paris, the house I was staying in, and came to the countryside, quite a small place on the seashore, to stay with some friends who had a garden. Now, in that garden there was a lawn...where there were flowers and around it some trees. It was a fine place, very quiet, very silent. I lay on the grass, like this, flat on my stomach, my elbows in the grass, and then suddenly all the life of that Nature, all the life of that region between the subtle-physical and the most material vital, which is very living in plants and in Nature, all that region became all at once, suddenly, without any transition, absolutely living, intense, conscious, marvellous; and this was the result, wasn't it? of six months of work which had given nothing. I had not noticed anything; but just a little condition like that and the result was there!

*

For more than a year I applied myself to this kind of self-discipline [noting down dreams]. I noted down everything — a few words, just a little thing, an impression — and I tried to pass from one memory to another. At first it was not very fruitful, but at the end of about fourteen months I could follow, beginning from the end, all the movements, all the dreams right up to the beginning of the night. That puts you in such a conscious, continuously conscious state that finally I was not sleeping at all. My body lay stretched, deeply asleep, but there was no rest in the consciousness. The result was absolutely wonderful; you become conscious of the different phases of sleep, conscious absolutely of everything that happens there, to the least detail, then nothing can any longer escape your control.

*

Between eleven and thirteen a series of psychic and spiritual experiences revealed to me not only the existence of God but man's possibility of uniting with Him, of realising Him integrally in consciousness and action, of manifesting Him upon earth in a life divine. This, along with a practical discipline for its fulfilment, was given to me during my body's sleep by several teachers some of whom I met afterwards on the physical plane.

Later on, as the interior and exterior development proceeded, the spiritual and psychic relation with one of these beings became more and more clear and frequent; and although I knew little of the Indian philosophies and religions at that time I was led to call him Krishna, and henceforth I was aware that it was with him (whom I knew I should meet on earth one day) that the divine work was to be done.

When I was a child of about thirteen, for nearly a year every night as soon as I had gone to bed it seemed to me that I went out of my body and rose straight up above the house, then above the city, very high above. Then I used to see myself clad in a magnificent golden robe, much longer than myself; and as I rose higher, the robe would stretch, spreading out in a circle around me to form a kind of immense roof over the city. Then I would see men, women, children, old men, the sick, the unfortunate coming out from every side; they would gather under the outspread robe, begging for help, telling of their miseries, their suffering, their hardships. In reply, the robe, supple and alive, would extend towards each one of them individually, and as soon as they had touched it, they were comforted or healed, and went back into their bodies happier and stronger than they had come out of them. Nothing seemed more beautiful to me, nothing could make me happier; and all the activities of the day seemed dull and colourless and without any real life, beside this activity of the night which was the true life for me. Often while I was rising up in this way, I used to see at my left an old man, silent and still, who looked at me with kindly affection and encouraged me by his presence. This old man, dressed in a long dark purple robe, was the personification — as I came to know later — of him who is called the Man of Sorrows.

*

Once when I was walking in the mountains, I was on a path where there was only room for one — on one side the precipice, on the other sheer rock. There were three children behind me and a fourth person bringing up the rear. I was leading. The path ran along the edge of the rock; we could not see where we were going — and besides it was very dangerous; if anyone had slipped, he would have been over the edge. I was walking in front when suddenly I saw, with other eyes than these — although I was watching my steps carefully — I saw a snake, there, on the rock, waiting on the other side. Then I took one step, gently, and indeed on the other side there was a snake. That spared me the shock of surprise, because I had seen and I was advancing cautiously; and as there was no shock of surprise, I was able to tell the children without giving them a shock, "Stop, keep quiet, don't stir." If there had been a shock, something might have happened. The snake had heard a noise, it was already coiled and on the defensive in front of its hole, with its head swaying — it was a viper. This was in France. Nothing happened, whereas if there had been any confusion or commotion, anything could have happened.

*

[I shall tell you] the story of a very well-known painter...I knew him very well. For I was doing painting at that time and practically lived among the painters, all the well-known artists of the epoch. Now this painter was a very fine artist with a genuine inspiration and a remarkable technique; some of his works have become world-famous. He was painting at his very best, but he was extremely poor, to the extent of almost starving. For his paintings were not in vogue and did not sell. Dealers came, saw and went away; they were not pleased with his work. And yet the paintings were really good. So in those hard days, a dealer came at last to have a look at his works. He examined them all one by one and rejected them wholesale. As he was turning back and going away disappointed his eyes fell suddenly upon a canvas lying in a corner and he exclaimed: "There, there's the thing I wanted. There is the masterpiece. How much do you want for it? I shall take it." What was this great painting? It was a canvas on which the painter used to lay his paint scrapings! The dealer asked him to do more of such things and promised to buy the whole lot of them. Here was new painting and a genius! What else could the poor artist do but obey his master, the merchant; for he too had to live.

*

Once, in Paris, I was crossing the Boulevard Saint Michel.... I had decided that within a certain number of months I would achieve union with the psychic Presence, the inner Divine, and I no longer had any other thought, any other concern. I lived near the Luxembourg Gardens and every evening I used to walk there — but always deeply absorbed within. There is a kind of intersection there, and it is not a place to cross when one is deeply absorbed within; it was not very sensible. And so I was like that, I was walking, when I suddenly received a shock, as if I had received a blow, as if something had hit me, and I jumped back instinctively. And as soon as I had jumped back, a tram went past — it was the tram that I had felt at a little more than arm's length. It had touched the aura, the aura of protection — it was very strong at that time, I was deeply immersed in occultism and I knew how to keep it — the aura of protection had been hit and that had literally thrown me backwards, as if I had received a physical shock. And what insults from the driver!

The Mother
Paris, 1895-96

The Mother
Algeria, 1908

I jumped back just in time and the tram went by.

*

Between the age of nineteen and twenty, I had achieved conscious and constant union with the Divine Presence, and...I had done so *all by myself*, with *absolutely nobody* to help me, not even books! When I found out — a little later, Vivekananda's *Raja Yoga* came into my hands — it seemed so marvellous that someone was able to explain something to me. It enabled me to achieve in a few months something which I might have taken years to do.

I met a man — I was about twenty-one, twenty or twenty-one, I think — I met a man, an Indian, who came from here and who told me about the Gita. There was a translation, a rather poor one, and he advised me to read it. He gave me the key, his key — it was his own key. He told me, "Read the Gita, this translation of the Gita, which isn't up to much..." But it was the only one in French. At that time, I would not have been able to understand anything in any other language. Besides, the English translations are just as bad, and I did not have.... Sri Aurobindo had not yet written his own translation. The man said, "Read the Gita, and take Krishna as the symbol of the immanent Divine, the inner Divine." That was all he told me. He said, "Read it with this, with this knowledge, that in the Gita Krishna represents the immanent Divine, the Divine who is within you." But within a month all the work was done!

*

I knew this a very long time ago. Fifty years ago.... There was that occultist who later gave me lessons in occultism for two years. His wife was a wonderful clairvoyant and had an absolutely remarkable capacity — precisely — of transmitting forces. They lived in Tlemcen [in Algeria]. I was in Paris. I used to correspond with them. I had not yet met them at all. And then, one day, she sent me in a letter petals of the pomegranate flower, "Divine's Love". At that time I had not given the meaning to the flower. She sent me petals of the pomegranate flowers telling me that these petals were bringing me her protection and force.

Now, at that time I used to wear a chain with my watch. (Wrist-watches were not known then or there were very few.) And there was also a small eighteenth century magnifying-glass.... And so there were two lenses, you see, as in all reading-glasses; there were two lenses mounted on a small golden frame, and it was hanging from my chain. Now, between the two glasses I put these petals and I used to always carry this about with me, because I wanted to keep it with me; you see, I trusted this lady and knew she had power. I wanted to keep this with me, and I always felt a kind of energy, warmth, confidence, force which came from that thing...I did not think about it, you see, but I felt it like that.

And then, one day, suddenly I felt quite depleted, as though a support that was there had gone. Something very unpleasant. I said, "It is strange, what has happened? Nothing really unpleasant has happened to me. Why do I feel like this, so empty, emptied of energy?" And in the evening, when I took off my watch and chain, I noticed that one of the samll glasses had come off and all the petals were gone. There was not one petal left. Then I really knew that they carried a considerable charge of power, for I had felt the difference without even knowing the reason. I didn't know the reason and it had made a considerable difference. So it was after this that I saw how one could use flowers to charge them with forces. They are extremely receptive.

*

Madame X was born on the Isle of Wight and she lived in Tlemcen with her husband who was a great occultist. Madame X herself was an occultist of great powers, a remarkable clairvoyant, and she had mediumistic qualities. Her powers were quite exceptional; she had received an extremely complete and rigorous training and she could exteriorise herself, that is, bring out of her material body a subtle body, in full consciousness, and do it twelve times in succession. That is, she could pass consciously from one state of being to another, live there as consciously as in her physical body, and then again put that subtler body into trance, exteriorise herself from it, and so on twelve times successively, to the extreme limit of the world of forms.... I shall speak to you about that later, when you can understand better what I am talking about. But I am going to tell you about some small incidents I saw when I was in Tlemcen myself....

The incidents are of a more external kind, but very funny.

She was almost always in trance and she had trained her body so well that even when she was in trance, that is, when one or more parts of her being were exteriorised, the body had a life of its own and she could walk about and even attend to some small material occupations.... She did a great deal of work, for in her trances she could talk freely and she used to narrate what she saw, which was noted down and later formed a teaching — which has even been published. And because of all that and the occult work she was doing, she was often tired, in the sense that her body was tired and needed to recuperate its vitality in a very concrete way.

Now, one day when she was particularly tired, she told me, "You will see how I am going to recover my strength." She had plucked from her garden — it was not a garden, it was a vast estate with ancient olive trees, and fig trees such as I have never seen anywhere else, it was a real marvel, on a mountain-side, from the plain to almost half way up — and in this garden there were many lemon trees and orange trees... and grapefruit. Grapefruit has flowers which have an even better fragrance than orange blossoms — they are large flowers and she knew how to make an essence from them herself, she had given me a bottle — well, she had plucked a huge grapefruit like this, (*gesture*) very large and ripe, and she lay down on her bed and put the grapefruit on her solar plexus, here, (*gesture*) like this, holding it with both hands. She lay down and rested. She did not sleep, she rested. She told me, "Come back in an hour." An hour later I returned...and the grapefruit was as flat as a pancake. That meant that she had such a power to absorb vitality that she had absorbed all the life from the fruit and it had become soft and completely flat. And I saw that myself! You may try, you won't succeed!...

She also had the power to dematerialise and rematerialise things. And she never said anything, she did not boast, she did not say, "I am going to do something", she did not speak of anything; she just did it quietly. She did not attach much importance to these things, she knew they were just a proof that there are other forces than purely material ones.

When I used to go out in the evenings — towards the end of the afternoon I used to go for a walk with Monsieur X to see the countryside, go walking in the mountains, the neighbouring villages — I used to lock my door; it was a habit with me, I always locked my door. Madame X would rarely go out, for the reasons I have already mentioned, because she was in a trance most of the time and liked to stay at home. But when I returned from the walk and opened my door — which was locked, and therefore nobody could have entered — I would always find a kind of little garland of flowers on my pillow. They were flowers which grew in the garden, they are called *Belles de Nuit*; we have them here, they open in the evening and have a wonderful fragrance. There was a whole alley of them, with big bushes as high as this; they are remarkable flowers — I believe it's the same here — on the same bush there are different coloured flowers: yellow, red, mixed, violet. They are tiny flowers like...bluebells; no, rather like the convolvulus, but these grow on bushes — convolvulus is a creeper, these are bushes — we have some here in the garden. She always used to put some behind her ears, for they have a lovely smell, oh! delightfully beautiful. And so, she used to take a walk in the alley between these big bushes which were quite high, and she gathered flowers, and — when I came back, these flowers were in my room!... She never told me how she did it, but she certainly did not go in there. Once she said to me, "Were there no flowers in your room?" — "Ah! yes, indeed," I said. And that was all. Then I knew it was she who had put them there.

*

In 1912 a small group of seekers met regularly with the aim of gaining self-knowledge and self-mastery.

At the end of each session, a general question was set, which each member was to answer individually. These answers were read out at the next meeting. Then, to close the session, a small essay was read out. Here [is an extract from one of] the essays.

The general aim to be attained is the advent of a progressing universal harmony.

The means for attaining this aim, in regard to the earth, is the realisation of human unity through the awakening in all and the manifestation by all of the inner Divinity which is One.

In other words, — to create unity by founding the Kingdom of God which is within us all.

This, therefore, is the most useful work to be done:

(1) For each individually, to be conscious in himself of the Divine Presence and to identify himself with it.

(2) To individualise the states of being that were never till now conscious in man and, by that, to put the earth in connection with one or more of the fountains of universal force that are still sealed to it.

(3) To speak again to the world the eternal word under a new form adapted to its present mentality.

It will be the synthesis of all human knowledge.

(4) Collectively, to establish an ideal society in a propitious spot for the flowering of the new race, the race of the Sons of God.

*

[This was] written in 1912. Many of you were not yet born. It was a small group of about twelve people who met once a week. A subject was given; an answer was to be prepared for the following week. Each one brought along his little work. Generally, I too used to prepare a short paper and, at the end, I read it out....

The subject for the first meeting was: What is the aim to be achieved, the work to be done, the means of achievement?...

I did not know Sri Aurobindo at that time and he had not written anything yet....

> "For each individually, to be conscious in himself of the Divine Presence and to identify himself with it."

Yes, you do not understand? I have said it fifty thousand times already, haven't I?...

> "To individualise the states of being that were never till now conscious in man and, by that, to put the earth in connection with one or more of the fountains of universal force that are still sealed to it."

"To individualise the states of being that were never till now conscious in man", that is to say, there are superposed states of consciousness, and there are new regions which have never yet been manifested on earth, and which Sri Aurobindo called supramental. It is that, this was the same idea. That is, one must go into the depths or the heights of creation which have never been manifested upon earth, and become conscious of that, and manifest it on earth. Sri Aurobindo called it the Supermind. I simply say these are states of being which were never yet conscious in man (that is, that man has so far never been aware of them). One must get identified with them, then bring them into the outer consciousness, and manifest them in action. And then, I add (exactly what I foresaw — I did not know that Sri Aurobindo would do it, but still I foresaw that this had to be done):

> "To speak again to the world the eternal word under a new form adapted to its present mentality."

That is, the supreme Truth, Harmony. It was the whole programme of what Sri Aurobindo has done, and the method of doing the work on earth, and I had foreseen this in 1912. I met Sri Aurobindo for the first time in 1914, that is, two years later, and I had already made the whole programme.

> "Collectively, to establish an ideal society in a propitious spot for the flowering of the new race, the race of the Sons of God."

Question: Where did you decide to found the Ashram?
Where did I decide to do it?... I never decided anything at all! I had simply said that it had to be done. I did not have the least idea, except that I had a great desire to come to India. But still, I did not even know if it corresponded to something. I had decided nothing at all. Simply, I had seen that state, what had to be done.

*

Although my whole being is in theory consecrated to Thee, O Sublime Master, who art the life, the light and the love in all things, I still find it hard to carry out this consecration in detail. It has taken me several weeks to learn that the reason for this written meditation, its justification, lies in the very fact of addressing it daily to Thee. In this way I shall put into material shape each day a little of the conversation I have so often with Thee; I shall make my confession to Thee as well as it may be; not because I think I can tell Thee anything — for Thou art Thyself everything, but our artificial and exterior way of seeing and understanding is, if it may be so said, foreign to Thee, opposed to Thy nature. Still by turning towards Thee, by immersing myself in Thy light at the moment when I consider these things, little by little I shall see them more like what they really are, — until the day when, having made myself one in identity with Thee, I shall no more have anything to say to Thee, for then I shall be Thou. This is the goal that I would reach; towards this victory all my efforts will tend more and more. I aspire for the day when I can no longer say "I", for I shall be *Thou*.

Prayers and Meditations
2 November 1912

*

What a hymn of thanksgiving should I not be raising at each moment unto Thee! Everywhere and in everything around me Thou revealest Thyself and in me Thy Will and Consciousness express themselves always more and more clearly even to the point of my having almost entirely lost the gross illusion of "me" and "mine". If a few shadows, a few flaws can be seen in the great Light which manifests Thee, how shall they bear for long the marvellous brightness of Thy resplendent Love? This morning, the consciousness that I had of the way Thou art fashioning this being which was "I" can be roughly represented by a great diamond cut with regular geometrical facets, a diamond in its cohesion, firmness, pure limpidity, transparency, but a brilliant and radiant flame in its intense ever-progressing life. But it was something more, something better than all that, for nearly all sensation inner and outer was exceeded and that image only presented itself to my mind as I returned to conscious contact with the outer world.

It is Thou that makest the experience fertile, Thou who renderest life progressive, Thou who compellest the darkness to vanish in an instant before the Light, Thou who givest to Love all its power, Thou who everywhere raisest up matter in this ardent and wonderful aspiration, in this sublime thirst for Eternity.

Thou everywhere and always; nothing but *Thou* in the essence and in the manifestation.

O Shadow and Illusion, dissolve! O Suffering, fade and disappear! Lord Supreme, art Thou not there!

Prayers and Meditation
26 November 1912

*

In the year 1910 my husband came alone to Pondicherry where, under very interesting and peculiar circumstances he made the acquaintance of Sri Aurobindo. Since then we both strongly wished to return to India — the country which I had always cherished as my true mother-country. And in 1914 this joy was granted to us.

As soon as I saw Sri Aurobindo I recognised in him the well-known being whom I used to call Krishna.... And this is enough to explain why I am fully convinced that my place and my work are near him, in India.

It matters little that there are thousands of beings plunged in the densest ignorance. He whom we saw yesterday is on earth; his presence is enough to prove that a day will come when darkness shall be transformed into light, and Thy reign shall indeed be established upon earth.

Prayers and Meditations
30 March 1914
(*the day after the Mother met Sri Aurobindo*)

*

Suddenly the veil was rent, the horizon was disclosed — and before the clear vision my whole being threw itself at Thy feet in a great outburst of gratitude. Yet in spite of this deep and integral joy all was calm, all was peaceful with the peace of eternity.

I seem to have no more limits; there is no longer the perception of the body, no sensations, no feelings, no thoughts — a clear, pure, tranquil immensity penetrated with love and light, filled with an unspeakable beatitude is all that is there and that alone seems now to be myself, and this "myself" is so little the former "I", selfish and limited, that I cannot tell if it is I or Thou, O Lord, sublime Master of our destinies.

It is as though all were energy, courage, force, will, infinite sweetness, incomparable compassion....

Even more forcibly than during these last days the past is dead and as though buried under the rays of a new life.... Lightened of a great weight I present myself before Thee, O my divine Master, with all the simplicity, all the nudity of a child.... And still the one only thing I perceive is that calm and pure immensity....

Lord, Thou hast answered my prayer, Thou hast

granted me what I have asked from Thee; the "I" has disappeared, there is only a docile instrument put at Thy service, a centre of concentration and manifestation of Thy infinite and eternal rays; Thou hast taken my life and made it Thine; Thou hast taken my will and hast united it to Thine; Thou hast taken my love and identified it with Thine; Thou hast taken my thought and replaced it by Thy absolute consciousness.

The body, marvelling, bows its forehead in the dust in mute and submissive adoration.

And nothing else exists but Thou alone in the splendour of Thy immutable peace.

Prayers and Meditations
10 April 1914

*

This morning passing by a rapid experience from depth to depth, I was able, once again, as always, to identify my consciousness with Thine and to live no longer in aught but Thee; — indeed, it was Thou alone that was living, but immediately Thy will pulled my consciousness towards the exterior, towards the work to be done, and Thou saidst to me, "Be the instrument of which I have need." And is not this the last renunciation, to renounce identification with Thee, to renounce the sweet and pure joy of no longer distinguishing between Thee and me, the joy of knowing at each moment, not only with the intellect but by an integral experience, that Thou art the unique Reality and that all the rest is but appearance and illusion.

Prayers and Meditations
12 May 1914

*

I shall relate an experience of mine when I first met Sri Aurobindo in Pondicherry. I was in deep concentration, seeing things in the Supermind, things that were to be but which were somehow not manifesting. I told Sri Aurobindo what I had seen and asked him if they would manifest. He simply said, "Yes." And immediately I saw that the Supramental had touched the earth and was beginning to be realised! This was the first time I had witnessed the power to make real what is true.

*

It was at the time of the First World War, the early days of the First War. I was here. I was staying in the house on Dupleix Street, "Dupleix House". From the terrace of that house could be seen Sri Aurobindo's room, the one in the "Guest House". Sri Aurobindo was staying there. He had two rooms and the small terrace. And from the terrace of Dupleix House the terrace of the Guest House could be seen (I don't know if it can still be seen; that depends on the houses in between, but at that time it could be). And I used to sit on the terrace to meditate every morning, facing Sri Aurobindo's room. That day I was in my room, but looking at Sri Aurobindo's room through a small window. I was in meditation but my eyes were open. I saw...Kali entering through my door; I said to her: "What do you want?" And she was dancing, a truly savage dance. She told me: "Paris is taken, Paris will be destroyed." We used to have no news, it was just at the beginning of the war. I was in meditation; I turned towards her and told her: "No, Paris will not be taken" and "Paris will be saved", quietly, just like this, but with a certain force. She made a face and went away. And the next day, we had the "dispatch" (in those days the radio was not yet there, we had telegraph messages, "dispatches", which were proclaimed, posted on the government-house door), we had the news that the Germans had been marching upon Paris, that Paris was not defended: the way was quite open, they had to advance only a few kilometers more and they would have entered the city. And when they saw that the road was free, that there was nobody to oppose them, they got it into their heads that it was an ambush, that a trap had been set for them! So they turned round and went back. And when the French armies saw that, naturally they gave chase and caught them, and there was a battle — it was the decisive battle. They were stopped. Well, evidently it was that. It was translated in this way; when I said to Kali, "No", they were panic-stricken. They turned back. Otherwise, if they had continued to advance it would have been all over.

*

In this formidable disorder and terrible destruction can be seen a great working, a necessary toil preparing the earth for a new sowing which will rise in marvellous spikes of grain and give to the world the shining harvest of a new race.... The vision is clear and precise, the plan of Thy divine law so plainly traced that peace has come back and installed itself in the hearts of the workers. There are no more doubts and hesitations, no longer any anguish or impatience. There is only the grand straight line of the work eternally accomplishing itself in spite of all, against all, despite all contrary appearances and illusory detours. These physical personalities, moments unseizable in the infinite Becoming, know that they will have made humanity take one farther step, infallibly and without care for the inevitable results, whatever be the apparent momentary consequences: they unite themselves with Thee, O Master eternal, they unite themselves with Thee, O Mother universal, and in this double identity with That which is beyond and That which is all the manifestation they taste the infinite joy of the perfect certitude.

> Peace, peace in all the world....
> War is an appearance,
> Turmoil is an illusion,
> Peace is there, immutable peace.

Mother, sweet Mother who I am, Thou art at once the destroyer and the builder.

The whole universe lives in Thy breast with all its life innumerable and Thou livest in Thy immensity in the least of its atoms.

Prayers and Meditations
31 August 1914

*

It was in 1914 that the identification with the Universal Mother took place, the identification of the physical consciousness with her. Of course, I knew before this that I was the Mother, but complete identification took place only in 1914.

*

I have visited trains, each one bringing between five and six hundred wounded from the front. It is a moving sight, not so much because of all that these unfortunate men are suffering, but above all because of the noble manner in which most of them bear their sufferings. Their soul shines through their eyes, the slightest contact with the deeper forces awakens it. And from the intensity, the fullness of the powers of true love which could, in their presence, be manifested in perfect silence, it was easy to realise the value of their receptivity....

And then the whole being, in a vast and luminous and objectless ecstasy, ceases to be "a being" and becomes the Boundless. And in the silence of contemplation the mentality knows that all these diverse constructions which present themselves to it are part of a whole which will be given to it to manifest progressively, perhaps through the medium of several bodily instruments. And the simultaneous vision of That which is and that which is becoming takes hold of this consciousness and does not leave it for many hours, hours ever more frequent and lasting.

*

In [Japan], for each season there are known sites. For instance, in autumn leaves become red; they have large numbers of maple-trees (the leaves of the maple turn into all the shades of the most vivid red in autumn, it is absolutely marvellous), so they arrange a place near a temple, for instance, on the top of a hill, and the entire hill is covered with maples. There is a stairway which climbs straight up, almost like a ladder, from the base to the top, and it is so steep that one cannot see what is at the top, one gets the feeling of a ladder rising to the skies — a stone stairway, very well made, rising steeply and seeming to lose itself in the sky — clouds pass, and both the sides of the hill are covered with maples, and these maples have the most magnificent colours you could ever imagine. Well, an artist who goes there will experience an emotion of absolutely exceptional, marvellous beauty....

Almost all — the most beautiful, the most striking [sites] — I had seen in vision in France; and yet I had not seen any pictures or photographs of Japan, I knew nothing of Japan. And I had seen these landscapes without human beings, nothing but the landscape, quite pure, like that, and it had seemed to me they were visions of a world other than the physical; they seemed to me too beautiful for the physical world, too perfectly beautiful. Particularly I used to see very often those stairs rising straight up into the sky; in my vision there was the impression of climbing straight up, straight up, and as though one could go on climbing, climbing, climbing.... It had struck me, and the first time I saw this in Nature down there, I understood that I had already seen it in France before having known anything about Japan.

*

A deep concentration seized on me, and I perceived that I was identifying myself with a single cherry-blossom, then through it with all cherry-blossoms, and, as I descended deeper in the consciousnss, following a stream of bluish force, I became suddenly the cherry-tree itself, stretching towards the sky like so many arms its innumerable branches laden with their sacrifice of flowers. Then I heard distinctly this sentence:

"Thus hast thou made thyself one with the soul of the cherry-trees and so thou canst take note that it is the Divine who makes the offering of this flower-prayer to heaven."

When I had written it, all was effaced; but now the blood of the cherry-tree flows in my veins and with it flows an incomparable peace and force. What difference is there between the human body and the body of a tree? In truth, there is none: the consciousness which animates them is identically the same.

Then the cherry-tree whispered in my ear:

"It is in the cherry-blossom that lies the remedy for the disorders of the spring."

Prayers and Meditations
7 April 1917

*

I was in Japan. It was at the beginning of January 1919. Anyway, it was the time when a terrible flu raged there in the whole of Japan, which killed hundreds of thousands of people. It was one of those epidemics the like of which is rarely seen. In Tokyo, every day there were hundreds and hundreds of new cases.... Now, it so happened I was living with someone who never ceased troubling me: "But what is this disease? What is there behind this disease?" What I was doing, you know, was simply to cover myself with my force, my protection so as not to catch it and I did not think of it any more and continued doing my work. Nothing happened and I was not thinking of it. But constantly I heard: "What is this? Oh, I would like to know what is there behind this illness. But could you not tell me what this illness is, why it is there?..." etc. One day I was called to the other end of the town by a young woman whom I knew and who wished to introduce me to some friends and show me certain things: I do not remember now what exactly was the matter, but anyway I had to cross the whole town in a tram-car. And I was in the tram and seeing these people with masks on their noses, and then there was in the atmosphere this constant fear, and so there came a suggestion to me; I began to ask myself: "Truly, what is this illness? What are the forces that are in this illness?..." I came to the house, I passed an hour there and I returned. And I returned with a terrible fever. I had caught it.... The doctor was called (it was not I who called him), the doctor was called and he told me: "I must absolutely give you this medicine." It was one of the best medicines for the fever, he had just a little (all their stocks were exhausted, everyone was taking it); he said: "I have still a few packets, I shall give you some" — "I beg of you, do not give it to me, I won't take it. Keep it for someone who has faith in it and will take it." He was quite disgusted: "It was no use my coming here." So I said: "Perhaps it was no use!" And I remained in my bed, with my fever, a violent fever. All the while I was asking myself: "What is this illness? Why is it there? What is there behind it?..." At the end of the second day, as I was lying all alone, I saw clearly a being, with a part of the head cut off, in a military uniform (or the remains of a military uniform) approaching me and suddenly flingling himself upon my chest, with that half a head to suck my force. I took a good look, then realised that I was about to die. He was drawing all my life out (for I must tell you that people were dying of pneumonia in three days). I was completely nailed to the bed, without movement, in a deep trance. I could no longer stir and he was pulling. I thought: now it is the end. Then I called on my occult power, I gave a big fight and I succeeded in turning him back so that he could not stay there any longer. And I woke up....

When someone came to see me, I asked to be left alone, I lay quietly in my bed and I passed two or three days absolutely quiet, in concentration, with my consciousness. Subsequently, a friend of ours (a Japanese, a very good friend) came and told me:"Ah! you were ill? So what I thought was true.... Just imagine for the last two or three days, there hasn't been a single new case of illness in the town and most of the people who were ill have been cured and the number of deaths has become almost negligible, and now it is all over. The illness is wholly under control." Then I narrated what had happened to me and he went and narrated it to everybody. They even published articles about it in the papers.

*

I belong to no nation, no civilisation, no society, no race, but to the Divine.

I obey no master, no ruler, no law, no social convention, but the Divine.

To Him I have surrendered all, will, Life and Self; for Him I am ready to give all my blood, drop by drop, if such is His will, with complete joy; and nothing in his service can be sacrifice, for all is perfect delight.

Written in Japan — February 1920

*

When I came from Japan, I was on the boat, at sea, not expecting anything (I was of course busy with the inner life, but I was living physically on the boat), when all of a sudden, abruptly, about two nautical miles from Pondicherry, the quality, I may even say the physical quality of the atmosphere, of the air, changed so much that I knew we were entering the aura of Sri Aurobindo. It was a *physical* experience and I guarantee that whoever has a sufficiently awakened consciousness can feel the same thing.

*

After granting me the joy which surpasses all expression, Thou hast sent me, O my beloved Lord, the struggle, the ordeal and on this too I have smiled as on one of Thy precious messengers. Before, I dreaded the conflict, for it hurt in me the love of harmony and peace. But now, O my God, I welcome it with gladness: it is one among the forms of Thy action, one of the best means for bringing back to light some elements of the work which might otherwise have been forgotten, and it carries with it a sense of amplitude, of complexity, of power. And even as I have seen Thee, resplendent, exciting the conflict, so also it is Thou whom I see unravelling the entanglement of events and jarring tendencies and winning in the end the victory over all that strives to veil Thy light and Thy power: for out of the struggle it is a more perfect realisation of Thyself that must arise.

Prayers and Meditations
22 June 1920

*

One day — every day I used to meditate with Sri Aurobindo: he used to sit on one side of a table and I on the other, on the veranda — and one day in this way, in meditation, I entered (how to put it?...), I went up very high, entered very deep or came out of myself (well, whatever one may say does not express what happened, these are merely ways of speaking), I reached a place or a state of consciousness from which I told Sri Aurobindo just casually and quite simply: "India is free." It was in 1920. Then he put to me a question: "How?" And I answered him: "Without any fight, without a battle, without a revolution. The English themselves will leave, for the condition of the world will be such that they won't be able to do anything else except go away."

It was *done*. I spoke in the future when he asked me the question, but there where I had seen, I said, India *is* free, it was a fact. Now, India was not free at that time: it was 1920. Yet it was there, it had been done. And it happened in 1947. That is to say, from the external physical point of view I saw it twenty-seven years in advance. But it had been done.

*

At the beginning of my present earthly existence I came into contact with many people who said that they had a great inner aspiration, an urge towards something deeper and truer, but that they were tied down, subjected, slaves to that brutal necessity of earning their living, and that this weighed them down so much, took up so much of their time and energy that they could not engage in any other activity, inner or outer. I heard this very often, I saw many poor people — I don't mean poor from the monetary point of view, but poor because they felt imprisoned in a material necessity, narrow and deadening.

I was very young at that time, and I always used to tell myself that if ever I could do it, I would try to create a little world — oh! quite a small one, but still...a small world where people would be able to live without having to be preoccupied with food and lodging and clothing and the imperative necessities of life, so as to see whether all the energies freed by this certainty of a secure material living would turn spontaneously towards the divine life and the inner realisation.

Well, towards the middle of my life — at least, what is usually the middle of a human life — the means was given to me and I could realise this, that is, create such conditions of life.

*

I remembered something that had happened.... I think I remember rightly, in 1926.

Sri Aurobindo had given me charge of the outer work because he wanted to withdraw into concentration in order to hasten the manifestation of the supramental consciousness and he had announced to the few people who were there that he was entrusting me with helping and guiding them; that I would remain in contact with him, naturally, and that through me he would do the work. Suddenly, immediately, things took a certain shape: a very brilliant creation was worked out in extraordinary detail, with marvellous experiences, contacts with divine beings, and all kinds of manifestations which are considered miraculous. Experiences followed one upon another, and, well, things were unfolding altogether brilliantly and...I must say, in an extremely interesting way.

One day, I went as usual to relate to Sri Aurobindo what had been happening — we had come to something really very interesting, and perhaps I showed a little enthusiasm in my account of what had taken place — then Sri Aurobindo looked at me...and said: "Yes, this is an Overmind creation. It is very interesting, very well done. You will perform miracles which will make you famous throughout the world, you will be able to turn all events on earth topsy-turvy, indeed,"... and then he smiled and said: "It will be a *great* success. But it is an Overmind creation. And it is not success that we want; we want to establish the Supermind on earth. One must know how to renounce immediate success in order to create the new world, the supramental world in its integrality."

With my inner consciousness I understood immediately: a few hours later the creation was gone.... And from that moment we started anew on other bases.

*

O my Lord, my sweet Master, for the accomplishment of Thy work I have sunk down into the unfathomable depths of Matter, I have touched with my finger the horror of the falsehood and the inconscience, I have reached the seat of oblivion and a supreme obscurity. But in my heart was the Remembrance, from my heart there leaped the call which could arrive to Thee: "Lord, Lord, everywhere Thy enemies appear triumphant; falsehood is the monarch of the world; life without Thee is a death, a perpetual hell; doubt has usurped the place of Hope and revolt has pushed out submission; Faith is spent, Gratitude is not born; blind passions and murderous instincts and a guilty weakness have covered and stifled Thy sweet law of love. Lord, wilt Thou permit Thy enemies to prevail, falsehood and ugliness and suffering to triumph? Lord, give the command to conquer and victory will be there. I know we are unworthy, I know the world is not yet ready. But I cry to Thee with an absolute faith in Thy Grace and I know that Thy Grace will save."

Thus, my prayer rushed up towards Thee; and, from the depths of the abyss, I beheld Thee in Thy radiant splendour; Thou didst appear and Thou saidst to me: "Lose not courage, be firm, be confident, — I COME."

Prayers and Meditations
24 November 1931

*

29 February 1956

During the Common Meditation on Wednesday

This evening the Divine Presence, concrete and material, was there present amongst you. I had a form of living gold, bigger than the universe, and I was facing a huge and massive golden door which separated the world from the Divine.

As I looked at the door, I knew and willed, in a single movement of consciousness, that *"the time has come"*, and lifting with both hands a mighty golden hammer I struck one blow, one single blow on the door and the door was shattered to pieces.

Then the supramental Light and Force and Consciousness rushed down upon earth in an uninterrupted flow.

*

The manifestation of the Supramental upon earth is no more a promise but a living fact, a reality.

It is at work here, and one day will come when the most blind, the most unconscious, even the most unwilling shall be obliged to recognise it.

*

The supramental world exists permanently and I am there permanently in a supramental body. I had the proof of this even today [3 February 1958] when my earth consciousness went there and remained there consciously between two and three o'clock in the afternoon. Now, I know that what is lacking for the two worlds to unite in a constant and conscious relation, is an intermediate zone between the physical world as it is and the supramental world as it is. This zone remains to be built, both in the individual consciousness and the objective world, and it is being built....

I was on a huge boat which was a symbolic representation of the place where this work is going on. This boat, as large as a city, is fully organised, and it had certainly already been functioning for some time, for its organisation was complete. It is the place where people who are destined for the supramental life are trained....

This immense ship had just reached the shore of the supramental world and a first group of people who were destined to become the future inhabitants of this supramental world were to disembark. Everything had been arranged for this first landing.... I was in charge of the whole thing from the beginning and all the time. I had prepared all the groups myself....

When I came back, simultaneously with the recollection of the experience I knew that the supramental world is permanent, that my presence there is permanent, and that only a missing link was necessary for the connection to be made in the consciousness and the substance, and it is this link which is now being forged.

*

There is only one thing of which I am absolutely sure, and that is *who I am*. Sri Aurobindo also knew it and declared it. Even the doubts of the whole of humanity would change nothing to this fact.

But another fact is not so certain — it is the usefulness of my being here in a body, doing the work I am doing. It is not out of any personal urge that I am doing it. Sri Aurobindo told me to do it and that is why I do it as a sacred duty in obedience to the dictates of the Supreme.

Time will reveal how far earth has benefited through it.

*

Question: Why did you come like us? Why did you not come as you truly are?

Because if I did not come like you, I could never be close to you and I would not be able to tell you: "Become what I am."

*

While looking at Sri Aurobindo's Samadhi:

I do not want to be worshipped. I have come to work, not to be worshipped; let them worship Thee to their heart's content and leave me, silent and hidden, to do my work undisturbed — and of all veils the body is the best.

*

It will be said of me: "She was ambitious, she wanted to transform the world." But the world does not want to be transformed except by a very long and slow process, so slow that the change cannot be perceptible from one generation to the other.

I find that Nature delays and wastes. But she finds that I am too much in a hurry and too troublesome and exacting.

Let me write down all I have to say; let me foretell all that will be done, and then, if no one finds that I am doing it properly, then I shall retire and leave the others to do it.

*

I am here because my body has been given for the first attempts at transformation. Sri Aurobindo said it to me. Well I am doing it.

*

When in your heart and thought you will make no difference between Sri Aurobindo and me, when to think of Sri Aurobindo will be to think of me and to think of me will mean to think of Sri Aurobindo inevitably, when to see one will mean inevitably to see the other, like *one and the same Person*, — then you will know that you begin to be open to the supramental force and consciousness.

*

Without him, I exist not;
without me, he is unmanifest.

*

I came to India to meet Sri Aurobindo; I remained in India to live with Sri Aurobindo. When he left his body, I continued to live here in order to do his work which is by serving the Truth and enlightening mankind, to hasten the rule of the Divine's Love upon earth.

*

Since the beginning of the earth, wherever and whenever there was the possibility of manifesting a ray of consciousness, I was there.

REFERENCES

The texts of this book (with two exceptions) are published in the sixteen volumes of the Mother's Collected Works, issued by the Sri Aurobindo Ashram, Pondicherry.

Volume	Title
1	*Prayers and Meditations*
2	*Words of Long Ago*
3	*Questions and Answers*
4	*Questions and Answers 1950-51*
5	*Questions and Answers 1953*
6	*Questions and Answers 1954*
7	*Questions and Answers 1955*
8	*Questions and Answers 1956*
9	*Questions and Answers 1957-58*
10	*On Thoughts and Aphorisms*
11	*Notes on the Way*
12	*On Education*
13	*Words of the Mother* [I]
14	*Words of the Mother* [II]
15	*Words of the Mother* [III]
16	*Some Answers from the Mother*

Page	Reference	Page	Reference
	Vol. 13, p. 45	24	Vol. 1, p. 138
1a	Vol. 13, pp. 38-39	25a	Vol. 3, p. 141
1b	*Mother India*, Feb. 1975, p. 95 (report)	25b	Vol. 6, pp. 68-69
		26	Vol. 1, pp. 233-34
1c	Vol. 5, pp. 139-40	27a	*Mother India*, Feb. 1975, p. 95 (report)
2	Vol. 5, pp. 198-200		
3a	Vol. 6, p. 166	27b	Vol. 2, pp. 137-38
3b	Vol. 16, p. 121	28	Vol. 4, pp. 306-07, 319
3c	Vol. 12, p. 157		
4a	Vol. 4, p. 42	29	Vol. 1, p. 359
4b	Vol. 6, p. 19	30	Vol. 5, pp. 182-85
5	Vol. 8, pp. 117-19	32a	Vol. 13, pp. 37-38
6	Vol. 6, pp. 40-42	32b	Vol. 4, p. 223
7	Vol. 6, pp. 186-87	33a	Vol. 1, p. 373
8	Vol. 4, p. 62	33b	Vol. 5, p. 190
9	Vol. 13, p. 39	34	Vol. 8, pp. 161-62
10a	Vol. 1, p. 81	35	Vol. 9, pp. 147-48
10b	Vol. 10, pp. 131-32	36	Vol. 1, p. 376
11	Vol. 7	37a	Vol. 15, p. 102
12	Vol. 10, pp. 132-33	37b	Vol. 15, p. 104
13a	Vol. 6, p. 298	38	Vol. 9, pp. 271-76
13b	Vol. 6, pp. 229-30	39a	Vol. 13, p. 47
15	Vol. 9, pp. 58-61	39b	Vol. 13, pp. 52-53
18a	Vol. 5, pp. 352, 354-56	39c	Vol. 13, pp. 45-46
		40a	Vol. 13, pp. 49-50
20	Vol. 1, p. 1	40b	Vol. 11, p. 308
21	Vol. 1, p. 5	40c	Vol. 13, p. 32
22	Vol. 13, p. 39	40	Vol. 13, p. 32
23a	Vol. 1, p. 113	40e	Vol. 13, p. 45
23b	Vol. 1, pp. 122-23	41	Vol. 13, p. 37

CHRONOLOGY

Some incidents in the Mother's external life:

1878	21 February. Born as Mirra Alfassa in Paris. Daughter of Maurice Alfassa (born in Adrianople, Turkey, in 1843) and Mathilde Ismaloun (born in Alexandria, Egypt, in 1857). Maurice, a banker, his wife and son (Matteo, born in Alexandria in 1876) had emigrated to France in 1877.
c.1892	At age 14 sent to a studio to learn painting and drawing; later studies at the Académie Julian and exhibits at the Paris Salon.
1893	Writes "The Path of Later On".
1906	Voyages to Tlemcen, Algeria, to study occultism with Max Théon and his wife.
1907	Voyages again to Tlemcen, Algeria.
1911-13	Gives many talks to various groups in Paris.
1912	First of the *Prayers and Meditations*, extracts from the Mother's spiritual journal begun in 1911.
1914	8 March. Departure for India. 29 March. Arrival in Pondicherry. Meeting with Sri Aurobindo. 15 August. First issue of the *Arya*; the Mother helps to edit its French edition.
1915	22 February. Departure from Pondicherry for France.
1916	4 March. Departure from Paris. 14 March. Embarks at London for Japan.
1916-20	In Japan.
1920	24 April. Return to Pondicherry.

1926	24 November. Foundation of the Ashram.
1943	2 December. Opening of the Ashram School.
1949	21 February. First issue of the *Bulletin of Physical Education*, (later *Bulletin of Sri Aurobindo International Centre of Education*) in which many of the Mother's writings and talks are first published.
1951	24 April. Convention for the inauguration of the Sri Aurobindo University Centre (presently called Sri Aurobindo International Centre of Education).
1973	17 November. Mahasamadhi: the Mother leaves her body.
	20 November. The Mother's body placed in the Samadhi, the vault in the courtyard of the Ashram where Sri Aurobindo's body was laid in 1950.
1978	Centenary of the Mother's birth. Publication of her complete works.